BRING ME DUCK
Folk Tales and Anecdotes from Duck, N.C.

by Suzanne Tate
as told by Ruth Scarborough Tate

NAGS HEAD ART
Illustrations by James Melvin

Nags Head Art
P.O. Box 88
Nags Head, N.C. 27959

Library of Congress Catalog Number 86-60040
ISBN 0-9616344-0-5
Copyright © 1986 by Nags Head Art

Dedicated to Frank
who on Sunday walks with his Aunt Iva
lived and loved Duck to its fullest

RUTH SCARBOROUGH

Age 11

DOG CORNER TO DOWNTOWN DUCK ~

Here I am—Ruth Scarborough Tate—surrounded by business places in fast-changing Duck. In the 30's and 40's this part of Duck from the Methodist Church to Osprey Landing was known as Dog Corner from so many dogs—three to four at each house.

We used to have open range here and the dogs sometimes served a purpose—they would catch and hold the hogs when they were being rounded up. But the dogs were mostly good for nothing but aggravation!

DUCK POST OFFICE ~

Lloyd Toler who kept a little store gave the neighborhood of Duck its name and was the first Postmaster here.

In 1909 when Lloyd arrived at the landing with a tin box to set up the post office, my brother George [then a young boy] asked him what he had in the box. Lloyd answered, "A post office." George said, "I ain't never seen one of those. If I go down the road with you, will you show it to me?" Lloyd said that he would, and they went to the store to set it up.

Lloyd chose the name of Duck as we used to have many ducks and geese here. Papa [George Johnson Scarborough] and my brothers hunted during the winter season and sold the wildfowl. They were packed in barrels with ice and shipped to northern companies. I stenciled names of the companies on the barrels.

Good money was made by the hunting before the sale of wildfowl was outlawed in 1918. Ducks brought as much as five dollars per pair. Canvasbacks and redheads were the best sellers. Young boys could make a lot of money cripple-ducking—catching the ducks that had been shot but not killed—when they came in close to the sound shore. If a boy got up before daylight, he could make twenty-five dollars in a morning.

OLD SAYINGS ~

We have had some amusing sayings at Duck:
"The clouds look like a whirly gust of woodpeckers."
"It looks like bull, beef and onions" [when a bad time was coming up].
"Calmer than in an old cow's belly."
"You never know the luck of a lousy calf" [when something bad turns out to be good].
"He's so tight he'd skin a louse for his tallow."
"The sun doesn't shine on the same dog's arse everyday."
My Grandpa Harris said, "Coming a sou'coon" whenever he saw a bad-looking squall coming out of the southwest.
It was considered bad luck to brush sand out of the house after sunset.

THE OLD STORE ~

Ned Rogers owned the old store. It was built in the fall of 1932 after an older one on the soundfront was washed down by storm tides in March of 1932.
Many a tale was told sitting around in the old store, and entertain-

ment as well was found there. Theodore Beals loved to sit around the store just to start something or aggravate the young'uns. He would charge them a penny or a soft crab to hear him sing a song—"Won't you come with me my pretty little pink, won't you come with me my daisy?" From an old Civil War ditty, I think. Another song he sang was, "The three little kittens lost their mittens and they began to cry", and then he would meow like the kittens.

Theodore would start yawning while he was sitting around the store. In five minutes, he got everybody to yawning, and then he would laugh at them.

There was a custom that Theodore made sure was always followed. If any fisherman fell overboard, he had to treat everybody at the store to a 5 cent soda.

MOSQUITOES ～

The mosquitoes were so thick when I was a girl that we would build a fire in a dishpan using old shoes, dry cow manure or something else that smouldered or smoked a lot. We set it on the porch and sat downwind of it to keep the mosquitoes off of us.

In the summertime when it was hot, and there were lots of mosquitoes, we cooked food and put it in lard tins and went in the sound in boats to eat. The mosquitoes usually did not go very far out on the water — you were safe at one-half mile.

TRIP TO NORFOLK ～

It was quite an undertaking to go to Norfolk, Virginia when I was a young girl. First we went by boat across the sound to Currituck, and

7

then we walked to North River to catch a steamer to Elizabeth City. Sometimes we hired a horsecart to Snowden's Station [present-day Belcross, North Carolina]. From there we took a train to Norfolk. In the summertime when the windows of the train were open, we got covered with coal soot.

A SHOPPING TRIP ∼

The stores we had in the neighborhood sold only groceries when I was a girl, so if we wanted to buy ready-made clothes or things like that we usually had to walk eight miles to Kitty Hawk.

But one trip when I was about ten years old, I will remember as long as I live. My cousin Hannah and friend Dixie and I went by skiff to Martin's Point where a man loaned us a cart and mule to go to Kitty Hawk. We had a time with that mule as he just crept along—he wouldn't have moved faster if you had beat the hair off of him. We could have made it to Kitty Hawk in half the time if we had walked.

NICKNAMES ∼

The folks at Duck loved to tease and give one another nicknames. Some of the colorful names were Turkle-Toler, Shad, Buckshire, Po' Johnny, Jo-Rad, Doughboy and Nitchy-Gander.

My son Everett was called Po' Johnny which was the local name for a blue heron. Once when he was a little boy, he became very excited when he spotted a heron—a lot bigger than he was—along the sound shore.

"Po', Po', Po' Johnny," he stammered to Jack Beals who was walking by with a shotgun. Jack took his gun, sneaked down to the bird and laid it on him. I pot-fried it for supper, and Everett ate it. Afterwards Jack called Everett "Po' Johnny" whenever he saw him, and others followed suit for many years.

V-I-A ∼

Lloyd Toler was nicknamed V-I-A because he advertised "Ship your fish V-I-A the Toler way." He would drive a truck loaded with fish to Norfolk, Virginia which was a trip from daylight to dark in the 30's. First of all, you had to go out five miles of dirt road along the sound from Duck. When driving through Currituck, the boys threw pieces of ice from the fish truck at every person they saw. So on the next trip, they got hit with Irish potatoes. The farmers had decided to get even!

Lloyd had a seine at the beach one day that he insisted the men set although the sea was very rough. The net broke loose from the anchors and went off in a few minutes, and his brother, James Frost, said, "There she goes—V-I-A the Toler way!"

TURKLES ∼

One night the men were sitting around Lloyd Toler's store and they were talking about trapping turkles [turtles]. Lloyd, who always corrected everybody on his English, told his brother James to look up "turkle" in the dictionary, so James did. He loudly spelled "T-U-R-K-L-E, TURKLE," slamming the book shut and putting it back on the shelf.

A little later, Lloyd went to the dictionary and discovered James' deceit. "I didn't think that you would lie like that," he said to his brother, and they about got into a fight. From that day on, James was called "Turkle-Toler."

PIGTAIL BEALS ~

Garfine Beals kept a store at the landing in the late 20's and bought fish. He sold salt pork out of barrels—everything was weighed up in those days.

One day he went to Elizabeth City to buy salt pork, but when he got home and opened up one of the barrels, there was nothing but pigtails in it! Someone wrote up an article in the *Independent* [present-day *Daily Advance*] about it, and from then on, Garfine was called "Pigtail Beals."

PLENTY OF FOOD ~

There was plenty of food at Duck when I was growing up. The women had vegetables from the large gardens and fruit to can for the winter. They would put up 30 or 40 mason quart jars of peaches and figs in each household.

We had chicken and eggs and cows in the woods. When the cows were fresh, we had milk and butter. We had salt pork, hams, and homemade sausage. I poured water for my Grandma Harris to scrub the intestines of the hogs that were saved for sausage-making. She turned the skin on a stick—it was like silk. The jaw bones of the hog were all that we threw away.

We had salt fish in pork barrels and fresh fish when we wanted them. The fish were split for salting with the bones left in one side.

People lived off waterfowl as well as seafood. The men got 8 or 10 swans in a hunting trip—it was illegal [killing swans], but they went just the same. After picking and dressing a swan, Papa took an ax and cut it up into four pieces for salting. Salted swan made really good meat for soup or for seasoning collard greens and cornmeal dumplings.

There were smokehouses for hams and potato houses for sweet potatoes. A potato house was made by digging a hole in the ground, filling it full of pine straw and building a roof over it. The sweet potatoes stored in a potato house would sweeten like candy.

Windin' the black peas was done by the women to blow the trash and shells out after shelling peas. They spread the peas on a blanket and fanned it in the wind.

DIAPER DECOYS ~

In the summertime, there were birds of all kinds along the sound shore. So around dusk Papa would take a bucket of wet baby diapers and some sticks to the shore. He stuck the sticks in the shallow water and draped the diapers on the sticks for white heron decoys. The scoggins [herons] were everywhere flying by, and as soon as he killed enough for a meal, he picked up the baby diapers and went home.

MAKING ICE TEA ~

There were no power lines at Duck until the forties. To make ice tea for supper, the men went by boat to Ned Rogers' fish house [where the ice was brought by truck from Dare County Ice Company at Manteo]. They got a piece of ice, wrapped it up in an oil cloth jacket, and headed for home as fast as they could.

HAIRY-CANES ∿

We had no warning of hurricanes in the 30's and before. We had a lot of northeasters in late summer and fall which were probably hurricanes. If it blew real hard, folks at Duck would say, "It must have been a 'hairy-cane'."

The worst hurricanes in my memory came in 1933. The first one came in the last of August and washed everything off the beach. The second one came along and blew away everything the first one did not wash away. We sawed wood for years from blown down trees around the sound shore.

During one of these storms, Saul Whitson went to check on his beach seine and dory that he had left behind the grassy hills just behind the beach. He said that he looked up and saw a wave wash over the Coast Guard telephone poles. It picked him up and washed him to the high hills halfway across the beach to Duck. He hurried on home and said that he did not care what happened to his net and boat!

The same hurricane left so many lakes of ocean water between the beach and the high sand hills to the west that the young'uns used them for swimming holes the following summer.

The second hurricane had such high winds in it that it picked up Papa's net-house, ripped it off the pilings and dropped it a short distance away. It opened right up and the walls fell apart. I remember that the walls in our house moved in and out two or three inches when gusts of wind hit it and pushed the rain through the weatherboarding. The house shook so much that the kerosene sloshed in the lamps!

FISHING INDUSTRY—20's ~

Old man Leary had a fishery where he packed fish and also kept fish alive. He had a sea cow in a long wooden tank. There were 100 families in the Duck neighborhood when I was a girl—some lived in fish camps on the beach. All of the families were involved in fishing one way or another.

The men were expert at dressing the fish. They could cut the belly, head and tail of herrings in one lick. There was a big business in selling salt fish especially to the farmers. The fish were salted down in kegs and would keep all winter.

Freight boats—the first one, I think, was called "Jones"—took the fish to Elizabeth City. The "Hattie Creef" also came into Duck.

CARP POUND—30's ~

Ned Rogers had a pound where he kept live carp. The pound was made out of 2 x 6 timbers sunk in the bottom of a deep part of the sound. There were two-inch spaces between the timbers to allow good circulation of water. The carp were in demand by Jewish people who came to get them in tank trucks so the fish could be kept alive.

The young'uns went swimming in the carp pound. When the pound got full of fish, they hit against the young'uns' legs as they were swimming.

The men bought 5 gallons of gas for one dollar and a quart of oil [sold in a glass bottle] for 25 cents to go to the islands north of Duck to catch carp. When they took them out of the water, they put them in a carp car which was an old skiff with holes cut in the sides for water circulation. Since the carp car floated level in the water, it was decked over so the fish could not get out.

The fishermen got 3 cents a pound for live carp. They were weighed carefully so as not to hurt or scratch them.

CRAB SHEDDING BUSINESS ~

During the Depression in the 30's, Carrie Beals and Caroline Rogers started at Duck the first crab shedding business in the county. They bought peelers [crabs that would soon shed] and kept them in large wooden floats until the crabs shed. They paid 1 cent each for peelers and 2 cents each for soft crabs. Almost all of the soft crabs were shipped to Norfolk on fish trucks.

Catching crabs was a good way for young'uns to make money, and some of them were especially good at it. Elmo Whitson probably caught the most of anybody.

The crabs were caught by wading along the sound shore. All that you needed was a dip net and a crab car tied to your waist and towed behind you.

Sometimes grown folks caught and sold crabs, too. We lived out of crabbing the summer of 1934. We made more than you could make at anything else at the time—one to four dollars per day.

A SWEET SURPRISE ~

Grandpa Harris and John Pugh fished together. On fishing trips they took their food in a wooden mincemeat bucket. One day they took a bucket of sugar by mistake!

When they opened it up and saw the sugar, Grandpa said, "Sweet Jesus, we're going home!" So they quit fishing right then and went home.

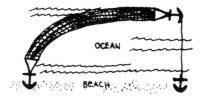

BEACH FISHING ~

It was a big thing to go to the beach to set a net. The fishing there was done with seines 300–600 yards long—usually by a crew of four men. Two or three men rowed a dory out to sea to set the seine. It was a special treat for the young'uns when they let them sit in the bow and go to sea with them.

The dory was pushed off from the beach through the breakers, and the net was set with one end anchored at the edge of the beach and the other end in a half moon shape anchored 300 or 400 yards at sea. A warp [line] was tied to the anchor at sea and rowed ashore so that the net could be pulled in without the men having to go to sea again.

Usually the net was set late in the afternoon or early evening and pulled in around daybreak the next morning. Sometimes the net was set back for the day and pulled in again in the early evening.

They caught all kinds of salt-water fish—spot, croaker, bluefish, speckled trout, grey trout and sea mullet. Fish were hauled across the beach to Duck by horsecart or oxcart before people owned any automobiles.

MENDING THE NETS ~

The nets we used were made of cotton, so they had to be dried before storing away or they would rot.

When the wind shifted northeast, and the ocean was too rough for fishing, the net was brought back to the neighborhood and stretched up on the backside of a house so that it could be mended. We used handcarved wooden net needles. It took several people two or three days to mend a 300–400 yard beach seine. The crew of three or four men would mend net and hire as many women as they could get.

The women were real good net-menders and could mend many a marsh [mesh of net]. All men in the neighborhood could mend net —even Lloyd Toler who had only one hand. Lloyd could tie bowties in his shoes as well!

In the 30's, we got 10 cents an hour for mending net. In later years we got 25 cents.

HAP ～

Manuel Santos—better known as "Hap"—was a native of the Azores. He came to live in the neighborhood in 1928 and stayed with us when we lived at Dan Scarborough's place.

Hap told us tales about the harsh life he lived in the Azores which was even harder than life in the 30's here. He said that everyone in his homeland had to serve in the army at the age of 21, and that they were paid only a penny a day.

Money was not much more plentiful at Duck during the Depression. Hap often told tales of how little money he had when he was fishing with a long-net crew. A long net is just like it sounds—a long net usually about a mile long pulled by two motor boats with another large skiff to carry the net.

Hap said that one time on a fishing trip the weather was bad, and they came into Manteo to tie up [their boats]. They ran out of groceries, and the whole crew could only come up with 10 cents, so they bought a pound of dried Navy beans with it. Since they did not have enough money to buy salt pork for seasoning, Hap put lard in a pan and burned it to get flavor for the beans.

Hap was a faithful churchgoer at the Methodist Church in the neighborhood. He always sat in the same place—in the back pew on the left side—and had a little switch which he tapped gently on each young'un as he or she arrived. Everyone knew he had been noticed and also was put on notice to behave.

Every week—between Sunday services—Hap had his own collection service going for the church. He carried what he called a "pogey-bag" everywhere he went and told the people—especially the ones who did not go to church—to feed the "pogey-bag." A quarter or any amount was all right with Hap, and then he would turn it in at the next Sunday service.

No one loved the young'uns better than Hap, and the young'uns loved him.

He often met the schoolbus so that he could give each one a little piece of candy. It didn't bust them open, but it was a treat just the same.

On the first day of school, Hap was always there to meet the schoolbus with a brand-new pencil for everyone.

When his white grapes—which he tended to with great care and pride—were ready, he let all the young'uns come to the grape arbor and pick and eat five grapes apiece at one time.

When Hap passed away in 1973 he left an unusual will. He directed that every young'un who attended his funeral be given a dollar bill. Some of those young'uns who are now grown—still have those dollars as a keepsake from their special friend.

SHARKS IN THE SOUND ~

When pigs went in the sound to eat watergrass, sharks ran them out. The hogs roamed free and fattened on the hard crabs [blue crabs] they caught in the sound. They would really fatten on them. There used to be a lot of crabs in the sound. In the "teens" you could catch five or six dozen soft crabs in 30 minutes.

Sheep also roamed free in the neighborhood back then. The sheep were sheared to get the wool for making long stockings for young'uns, gloves for menfolk, and scarves. First we washed the wool and dried it, and it had to be broken up and carded into rolls. Then we spun it and skeined it on "windin' blades" [a wooden device for skeining yarn]. The skein was tied in two or three places and dyed—some was left in the natural color. Red oak bark made a pretty dye. There were lots of red oaks in the woods—you could get all you wanted.

DIPPING THE CATTLE—20's ∼

Cattle were rounded up by the men on horseback. In hot weather you could see as many as one hundred cattle at a time cooling off in the sound. There was plenty of water for livestock to drink.

Every two or three weeks, they rounded up the cattle from the highway to Caffey's Inlet to run them through the dipping vat to kill fever ticks. The men enjoyed it better than going to a circus.

After running the cattle through the vat, each one was marked with a dab of green paint on its rump, so that they could keep track of the ones that had been dipped and those that had not.

One time a calf landed on its back in the vat. There was a holdup in driving the cattle through, and Andrew Scarborough had time to paint the steer's horns all green. Everybody had a good laugh about that!

Old man Leary had an old black cow that would hide during the roundups. So they tied a bell on her so that they could find her. But she was a slick cow as she would lay her head on the ground to keep the bell from ringing.

The whole beach [Outer Banks] was open range back then. We had fences around our homes to keep hogs from under the houses and livestock from rubbing—scratching themselves—against the houses and ruining the gardens.

When bridges and roads were built, a law was passed requiring all livestock to be fenced in. It was called the "no fence law" because folks no longer had to fence in their houses and gardens to keep the animals out.

Some of the people who had a lot of stock screamed and hollered and took their guns to the county courthouse at Manteo to protest the law, but the whole county had voted for it, and the law had to come sooner or later.

WOODCUTTIN'S ~

People in the neighborhood always helped one another. Everybody would gather up at Papa's house to cut his wood and then go on to someone else's house. They carried two gallons of whiskey to the woodcuttin'—it was more like a celebration than work.

DROWNDED LIQUOR ~

Around 1931 wooden cases of whiskey drifted ashore up and down the beach near Duck. Folks were very happy to find it and called it "drownded liquor."

Through the years bounty from the sea washed up—bananas, oranges and driftwood for building houses and barns. My Grandma Harris could carry three 16-foot boards across the beach on her hip!

OIL CLOTHES ~

Grandma Harris made oil clothes for the men at #11 Life Saving Station [Paul Gamiels Hill]. She used cotton ducking which was later painted with two or three coats of linseed oil that made the clothes real stiff and kept them from leaking. She also made hats called sou'westers that had a long brim in the back and a short one in front.

One of the duties of the surfmen was to go on patrol between lay houses halfway between life saving stations. In particularly bad weather, they would wrap themselves up in their carts and never have to tell their horses where to go. The horses were so used to the patrol that they knew right where to stop. The surfmen each had a key and when they met the other men on patrol, they used the keys to punch each other's clocks as proof that they had made the patrol.

EMERSON ROGERS' PLACE ～

In the family graveyard in front of their home, Emerson and "Med" [Maryland] Rogers buried two of their three children—Harriett and Charlie. They also buried their third one, Willie, in a little graveyard in the neighborhood. All died when they were young people. Folks used to have family graveyards everywhere.

Emerson's brother Johnny is also buried in the yard. He was "squlped" when a tree fell on him. When they were cutting down trees one day, Johnny ran in the wrong direction right under a falling tree.

Miss "Med" always wore long dresses and a felt hat with a large brim. She was never seen outside without wearing a hat. One time she was mending net, and the wind kept blowing up her dress. The next day she appeared with net leads—that she had beat flat—in the hem of her dress to hold it down in the wind!

NEW CHRISTMAS AND OLD CHRISTMAS ～

When I was young, December 25th—new Christmas—was a partying time at Duck. The partying began early as the men shot off their shotguns to wake the others up at daybreak, so they would get the eggnog made. The people started out before breakfast, going to each house to get a glass of eggnog. Some had nog without egg!

On the day before, the women cooked all day. They made thin pies on bright, thin pie-pans. Mama cooked one dozen coconut pies, one dozen sweet potato pies as well as two layer cakes, one lemon and one chocolate. The women in the other households did the same thing.

Old and young would start dancing in someone's livingroom, and they danced all night Christmas Eve. One man danced until all the buttons popped off his drawers. Uncle Dan could make an accordion talk.

Old Christmas on January 6th was celebrated just like a Sunday. There was no drinking, dancing or carousing. But pies were cooked on Christmas Eve, January 5th. Stockings were hung as at New Christmas, but the young'uns received no toys—these were received at New Christmas. The stocking were stuffed full of fruits and nuts. Grownups did not exchange gifts—the gifts were only for the young'uns.

People would see "signs" at Christmastime. The old people believed that while it was safe to take ashes out of the stove, it was bad luck to carry ashes outside during the period between Christmases. If you did, it was believed that you would soon carry out a dead person from your home.

SANCTIFIED MEETINGS ~

Early church meetings at Duck when I was little were called "sanctified meetings." These were held in the open on the sound during the day and into the night when lanterns were hung on net stakes for light.

People came from across the sound in solid swarms. They came in boatloads to attend the meetings and eat the dinners prepared by the women at Duck. Beef and hogs were killed, and women cooked all day on Saturdays and on Sunday mornings.

The visitors ate so much that the women did not have enough left to feed their own families. This went on for several years. Finally, the women told their husbands that they had had enough.

One woman, Lucinda Beals—who could cuss like a sailor—stopped some people who were crawling over her closed gate looking for their dinner. She firmly invited them to go back over the gate!

Sanctified meetings were lively get-togethers. The people leaped with their feet close together, two or three feet straight up in the air. At one of these meetings Caleb Toler testified, "I'm as good as Jesus Christ and gettin' better everyday!"

When Mama [Flaud Scarborough] heard that, she had heard enough. She picked up her bonnet and left the meeting, her frock tail popping.

SCHOOLHOUSE CHURCH ～

A group of people began meeting for church in the Duck school-house around 1917. After the children all went to Kitty Hawk a few years later, the building was turned into a Methodist Church.

One of the first preachers was W. A. Betts who always walked from Kitty Hawk to Duck to preach and would not accept a ride if offered one. He would not allow any manner of work on the Sabbath, so his family could not eat one mouthful of food except what was cooked from the day before.

Mr. Betts wore an old overcoat that was so long it frapped him on his heels when he walked. He would sit and make fun of you to your face, and one day Papa ran Mr. Betts out of the yard for making fun of him. Papa had cut off gum boots to make shoes out of them, and Mr. Betts said, "Be sure to wear those little shoes when you come to church." And Papa said, "See that gate—you better be gettin' out of it!"

BAPTISMS IN THE SOUND ～

In the 1930's there was a hell-fire and brimstone preacher by the name of Matthew Gardner. He frightened the young'uns and baptised many people in the sound. At the baptisms, the people's frocks were switching around them soaking wet.

When they came out of the sound, Gardner's wife walked to my porch steps and demanded a clean towel and a pan of water to wash her husband's feet. His foot-washing became a ritual every time he held baptisms in the sound.

At church services, Preacher Gardner screamed, "Sit there in your seats like blocks of stone and go straight to Hell." He also made remarks about the men fishing on Sunday. This caused Papa to clear his throat loudly, pick up his hat and leave in the middle of the service one day.

Mr. Gardner was also very unhappy that on Sundays, my son Everett and the King boys carried swill on an old flatbed truck from the Duck Transit Camp to Tom King's house for his hogs.

PREACHER SPIES ~

In 1940 just before World War II, two young men—blond and speaking perfect English—came walking down the beach and began holding long meetings at the church.

The people at Duck always believed that they were German spies. In any event, they knew little about preaching!

WITCHES AND PIRATES ~

A witch was supposed to have lived on the shoreside in a little camp. It was said that she could turn herself into a speckled hen. My Grandpa Harris said that he saw a speckled hen sitting in a bread tray floating by him one moonlight night in the sound.

Some of the fishermen were so convinced that she was a witch that they would not go fishing if she said that they would not catch any fish that day.

Still another witch was said to have been seen floating in an eggshell with a paddle in her hand.

Mama told us that Old Teach [Blackbeard] lived in the swamp next to the sand hills, so that we would stay away from a deep pond of water that was there. In some places the water was over our heads. But my cousin Levin Scarborough when he was not bigger than a grasshopper said, "I'll take my paddle and beat the Hell out of Old Teach." He and I paddled around in the pond in a little square-ended bateau.

At times when the wind was lightly to the east and especially in foggy weather, people said that you could hear Old Teach's drum go "Whoom, Whoom."

Levin's grandmother—when she was a little girl—saw pirates come ashore in a yawl from a big ship. She got so scared that she climbed a tree. After the pirates had buried a chest and left, she ran home to tell her folks about it. They all went back to the beach, but the tide had come in and washed all trace away of where the chest was buried.

Major and Steve Rogers told the story that they found a gallon bucket of money up on the sand hill just south of Duck. When Major said, "Would you look at the money!", the money disappeared.

Folks said you had to get buried money in your pocket before you said a word or it would disappear.

MAN WITHOUT A HEAD ～

Across from my house there used to be a cart path from the ocean. People said that a man without a head often came and stood there. He was most likely to appear after a shipwreck on the beach. They claimed that he was the ghost of Old Teach.

I never saw him, but my cousin Hannah said that he followed her up

24

the road one time. When she stopped and turned around, he disappeared.

HAUNTED HOUSE AT SLABTOWN ~

My brother George loved to tell tales. His favorite was about the haunted house at Slabtown where he and his wife Thelma lived for awhile.

When George and Thelma were sort of newlyweds, they lived upstairs over us at Corolla [20 miles north of Duck] where my husband Sam had gone to be a marsh guard for Whaleshead Club. George learned of a vacant house at Slabtown, six miles farther north up the beach and went to ask if he could rent it. But the man who owned it offered it to him free. He said, "George, if you can live in it, you're welcome to stay in it as long as you like. It's too much on my nerves—I can't stay in it."

George and Thelma went to live in the house and saw and heard many unexplained happenings. They said that you could hear a sewing machine running at one corner of the house when you were outside, but no one inside heard a thing. At other times from the outside it sounded like someone was tearing up the house with an ax, but nothing was touched when you went back inside.

And one day while Thelma's sister Sue was visiting, they were sitting in the kitchen eating the noon meal when they looked out of the window and saw a white horse prancing around in the garden. They all got up and ran out to chase the horse away. But they did not find a sign of the horse, a hoof print or a leaf touched although the garden was full of vegetables.

Sue had come to stay quite a spell, but George had to take her home before the first week was out because she was a nervous wreck. She had said that she was not afraid of anything!

25

LOST TREASURE AT MARTIN'S POINT CREEK ～

A man by the name of Hodges Gallop who owned his own schooner hauled lumber from his dock at Martin's Point Creek [three miles south of Duck] to the West Indies and returned with loads of sugar and coffee.

My brother George told the tale that Captain Gallop was in Baltimore one time during the Civil War when there was a great fire. The business people were afraid that their money would burn up, so they rolled their safes aboard Gallop's schooner for safekeeping. He was supposed to anchor in Baltimore harbor, but he was gone the next morning, headed for North Carolina. He ended up at Martin's Point Creek at his stone dock.

When he got there, Union troops were coming down the mainland [Currituck], and he needed to leave in a hurry. Since it was low tide, and his schooner was heavy with the safes, he decided to dump them in the deepest part of the creek, and he took off for the West Indies.

Nobody ever got the safes up again. Captain Gallop could not find them when he went back to look for them — they probably had sunk down in the mud.

Many years later, George one day felt something hard with a shoving pole, but had no way to dive down to check for the safes.

He got a diver to go look at the spot years after that, but it had silted up. So if his tale is true, the safes are still there under the mud at Martin's Point Creek.

TOMMY TATE'S TALE ～

My brother-in-law Tommy liked to tell the story about a witch who lived in a camp on the marsh near Duck. She often put a spell on hunters—telling them that they would not get any geese or ducks.

One day there was a goose that kept flying over the decoys of some hunters. When they blasted away at the goose, there was no effect on it, and they could hear the witch cackling back at her camp.

One of the hunters had heard that you could kill a witch with silver, so he cut up a dime and opened a shotgun shell and put the silver in there. When the goose came back, he killed it, and the witch who was leaning in her doorway eating a sweet potato fell out of the door stone dead.

Tommy always ended the tale by saying "And that's the damn truth."

KINGS OF THE SOUND ～

One time an undercover federal game warden hired Bill Riley Hines and Cecil O'Neal to take him out fire-lighting for swans, which was strictly against the law.

Fire-lighting was the practice of putting a lantern on the bow of a boat at night and pushing up to the birds while they were blinded by the light.

Bill and Cecil were both men of small stature, so when they were shoving up on the swans, Bill hollered to Cecil, "We're the Kings er the Sound, ain't we, Cees, old boy?" And Cecil replied, "Yup!"

The game warden handed each man a gun and said, "Boys, I can't see 'em very well—go ahead and shoot 'em for me." So they blasted away and killed him a boatload.

But when they arrived back at the dock, the game warden put handcuffs on both of the "Kings".

LIVE DECOYS ～

Geese and ducks were used for live decoys as late as in the 30's. When you opened the cages to take them to the blinds, they would crawl right in.

A metal rod was pushed in the bottom of the sound and a leather band with a brass ring fastened to it was placed around the leg of a bird to keep it from swimming off—although it was pretty tame from being fed. The rig was a neat job that did not bother the birds at all. The geese and ducks swam around in place and "talked" in the wildfowl.

The live decoys were valuable property—they were a lot of trouble to raise—and the hunters were careful not to harm them. They always shot birds in the air, but real sportsmen never shot a bird on the water anyway.

TURFING OUT ～

One evening between sunset and dark my brother George set out turfs [big chunks of marsh peat] in the shallow water of the sound for decoys for the evening fly of black ducks.

Archie Curles and Grissy Barco came shoving along in their boat and thought the turfs were real ducks, blasting them all to pieces. Folks never let them live it down!

POWDER RIDGE CLUB ～

Powder Ridge Club at Duck was a hunting club owned by a group of Wall Street brokers. My brother Lewis was the caretaker, and he and his wife Leona and family lived there in the 30's.

To go down the lane to the club, you had to put up with several feisty animals. First, three pairs of mean geese were setting in the lane. There was also "Old Jim," largest goose you ever saw that stuck out his neck like a snake and hissed and beat his wings against anyone who came near the nests.

Lewis' son Tink was so scared that he would run down the lane and go right over the gate like a shot out of a gun. My son Everett would run the lane while "Old Jim" chased him and the other geese joined in.

At one time there was a billy goat a third of the way of the lane that butted anybody that he caught up with. And at the end of the lane there was a big black lab, a biting dog named Sam Jones—a gift from a man by the name of Sam Jones. He would raise his bristles and act like he would tear you up.

When black Ann Susan came from across the sound to cook at Powder Ridge Club during the hunting season, every young'un came to look at her as black people were so rare at Duck. She stayed in a little house at the club.

Ann Susan could always find a scrap of food for Donovan, my nephew, and Everett. She didn't like green. One time Lewis was going to paint her house, and she said, "Please, Mr. Scarbo'—don't paint my house green—it's hard luck!"

LEONA SCARBOROUGH'S ROOSTER ~

My sister-in-law Leona had a buff-colored rooster that tackled anything that came along. He had two-inch spurs like extra toes on his feet.

Donovan and Everett got a stick one day and cornered him at the fence and knocked him out—they thought he was killed! The boys came back later, and the first thing they met was that rooster strutting around big as life.

Leona finally gave him away, as he was so mean.

LEWIS' BILLY GOAT ~

My brother Lewis had a white billy goat that climbed up on the hood of his convertible and ate a hole right over the driver's seat.

Lewis was so mad that he went for his gun to shoot the goat, but Leona tackled my brother and talked him out of it.

Later on, the goat got his horn caught in a hog-wire fence and was injured so badly that Lewis got his chance to shoot him.

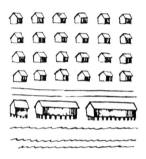

DUCK TRANSIT CAMP ~

In the 30's there was a camp run by the federal government in Duck Woods east of Martin's Point.

There were little square camps with four men to each building. Over a hundred men of all ages and from all walks of life stayed at the camp. The government fed them and paid them four or five dollars a week to build sand fences and plant grass all up and down the beach.

They had a large, long mess hall and a large canteen with several pool tables where they sold soft drinks, candy, ice cream and beer. The camp had its own generator, so they even had electricity.

The Transit Camp was a great thing for the people at Duck. The men were friendly and bought drinks and ice cream for the young'uns. Everyone in the neighborhood enjoyed moving pictures once a week at an outdoor theater at the camp. A whole bunch of us piled in trucks to go to the shows which were the first moving pictures people at Duck ever saw. During bad weather, they set up the projector in the mess hall.

When my son Eddie was only three or four years old, he regularly got up on a bench on our front porch to wave to the transit camp men as they were going by in a truck. They were on their way up to the beach to build sand fences. The men always yelled, "Hey, Bill" to Eddie and would throw out a roll of magazines for him.

BOMBING RANGE ~

A mile north of Duck, the Navy had big targets on the sand hills for a bombing range. They used the range over a period of about 20 years.

Emerson Rogers told a story about a preacher who came to eat Sunday dinner at his house. The preacher announced that his soul was right with the Lord, and that when the Lord called he was ready to go.

About that instant, the Navy started bombing with some of their "Tiny Tims" [large, loud, explosive bombs], and the preacher dived under the table!

DRUM FISHING ~

Our favorite sport in late summer and fall was to go hook and lining for drum [channel bass]. We first walked up the sandy shore north of Duck with the drum lines in our pockets to get bait.

We used small mullets that were killed with mullet fraps. A mullet frap had a heavy steel wire tied to one end of a stick that was frapped in the shallow water to kill the fish.

Then we walked barefooted one mile straight across to the ocean—there were no sand spurs, just clean sand hills—to throw out the drum lines.

A drum line was made of 50 yards of #24 white cotton twine, and it had eight 2-ounce net leads for a sinker and two 9 or 10-0 hooks on it.

We tied a 2-inch wooden toggle about six feet up from the sinker, so that the line could be swung over the head and thrown out in the ocean.

When a drum was hooked, we ran up on the beach until we pulled it out of the water. There were always bamboo poles lying on the beach where they had washed up, so we stuck a pole through the fish's gills. Then we swung it over a shoulder and toted the drum—weighing 40–50 pounds—back aross the sand hills to Duck.

BURYING THE DEAD ∽

There was no embalming of the dead at Duck until the 30's. We kept up the bodies for a day or two, but I have known of keeping them up for three or four days. The bodies sometimes smelled so bad that you could smell them when you went by the house on the road.

For shrouding the dead—fixing them up—the women got a pan of water, washed and sponged off the body and combed the hair. My husband Sam always sharpened up his straight razor and went to shave the men.

The bodies were soaked in camphor to keep down the odor. They were laid out on a bed and covered up in a sheet called their "windin' sheet."

The shroud was a long gown of bleached cotton all covered with embroidery. Older women made their own shrouds years before they died, putting them away until they were needed.

We sat up with the dead all night until they were buried. Miss Lucinda Beals said that she sat up by an old man who was laid out when a black cat jumped up and tried to scratch the sheet off his face. The cat was just "a 'furring"—probably attracted to the camphor. Miss Lucinda—who was not afraid of the devil himself—gave the cat a pitch out the door!

The men in the neighborhood built the coffins. All they were was a pine box that the women padded with a blanket and lined with bleached cotton. The men also built a wooden box to set the coffin in.

Levy Perry built his own coffin—he got in it and lay down and tried it out to see if it was the right size.

32

For the ones buried at Kitty Hawk, we carried them by horse and cart or by boat. If they were buried in the neighborhood, we used just a horse and cart.

Services were held in homes or outdoors—there were no church services. We always sang a hymn and laid on the grave wildflowers or flowers cut out of the yard. Everyone back then had chyrsanthemums that lasted all winter.

People also made their own tombstones which were logwood posts or heart pine.

LADIES' AID SOCIETY—30's ～

The women in the neighborhood used to hold bake sales and make quilts. They sat around in Ned Rogers store and dipped snuff while they worked.

On Saturdays in the summertime, they made homemade ice cream and sold it at the store. Every Christmas they bought oranges, apples, candies and nuts that were given away at the church to everyone. They also would go to Norfolk on a fish truck to buy Christmas gifts for every young'un in the neighborhood.

CAR CORNER—DUCK IN THE 80's ～

Duck has changed a lot, but I still enjoy living here—although cars have taken the place of dogs! Soon the cars will be thicker than the fleas on the dogs that used to be here at Dog Corner.

People ask me—what do I think of all the changes? I think that you can't stop the world from moving on. It's going to move on with or without you, so you might as well make the best of it!

PHOTO MEMORIES
Old & New

THE MEN AT #11 LIFE SAVING STATION
Paul Gamiels Hill—1914

PAPA & MAMA & CHILDREN
in front of old schoolhouse around 1906

MAMA & PAPA
turn of the century

RUTH—1906
Etta Scarborough made our fancy clothes

SAM & TOMMY TATE—20's
my husband & his half-brother

ELSIE & ETTA
SCARBOROUGH—40's
*Levin's daughter & mother
at old home place*

SUE BEALS—30's
she didn't like the haunted house

POWDER RIDGE CLUB—30's
whalebones decorated the front

LEWIS & LEONA
SCARBOROUGH & FAMILY
in front of Powder Ridge Club

LEWIS' CONVERTIBLE
that the goat ate the top of

IVA, DONOVAN
& EVERETT—1928
daughter, nephew & son with old Sport

DONOVAN, MILFORD & BOBBY
nephews & friend - no need for sand box at Duck

IVA WITH FRIEND
FRANCES—1938
eel pots in background

PEARL GARD AT DUCK POST OFFICE
Amy Wright was postmaster here from 1911–1941—then it was closed

PAPA WITH CARP—30's
he was a fisherman, hunter & storekeeper

BEACH FISHING — EARLY 50's
pushing off to set the net

BEACH FISHING — 50's
boating the net

BEACH FISHING — LATE 40's
pulling in net

BEACHFISHING—50's
bunting—pulling in last pocket of net

SAM & RUTH — SOMETIME IN 50's
mending net

CARRIE BEALS & RUTH — EARLY 50's
hanging net in lines

43

"HAP" — 50's
in trapping gear

DUCK ROAD by the shoreside — 50's
just a sandy trail

OUR LANDING HOUSE — 1954
where we stored nets

Photos taken August 23, 1985
courtesy of R. Porter Fay and photographer Paul S. Marley

EMERSON ROGERS' PLACE
with family graveyard

DUCK METHODIST CHURCH
gone but not forgotten

LEVIN SCARBOROUGH
carving his ducks

OLLIE & DAN SCARBOROUGH'S HOME FROM 1960-1980
*formerly Ned Roger's home place [built in 1932] where
hunting parties stayed—now gone for progress' sake*

GLOSSARY

A'FURRIN'—an animal scratching

BATEAU—small boat square-ended on each end

DORY—seagoing rowboat used in commercial fishing

DRUM—channel bass

DUCKING—lightweight canvas

FIRELIGHTING—illegal hunting practice of blinding animals with a light after dark

FRAPPED—flapped

GUM BOOTS—rubber boots

HAIRY-CANE—hurricane

HARD CRAB—unmolted stage of blue crab

LAY HOUSE—small hut halfway between life saving stations where surfmen on patrol met to punch each other's clocks

LAY IT ON HIM—to kill or catch fish or fowl

MARSH—mesh of net

PEELER—crab that will shed its shell within two weeks

POUND—large pen or corral used in commercial fishing

SANCTIFIED MEETING—church meeting

SCOGGIN—heron

SEINE—net

SHROUD—burial clothes

SIGN—supernatural happening

SKIFF—small boat

SOFT CRAB—molted stage of blue crab

SOU'COON—storm from southwest direction

SOU'WESTER—rainhat with large brim in back to keep water from running down collar

SQULPED—squashed

SURFMAN—man who rowed boats through surf at life saving station

SWILL—garbage

TURF—chunk of marsh peat

TURKLE—turtle

WARP—long rope